PEBBLE & I

John Fuller

Chatto & Windus

LONDON

Published by Chatto & Windus 2010

2 4 6 8 10 9 7 5 3 1

First published in Great Britain in 2010 by
Chatto & Windus
Random House, 20 Vauxhall Bridge Road,
London SW1V 2SA

www.rbooks.co.uk

Addresses for companies within The Random House Group Limited
can be found at:
www.randomhouse.co.uk/offices.htm

The Random House Group Limited Reg. No. 954009

A CIP catalogue record for this book
is available from the British Library

ISBN 9780701184919

The Random House Group Limited supports The Forest Stewardship Council (FSC),
the leading international forest certification organisation. All our titles that are
printed on Greenpeace approved FSC certified paper carry the FSC logo.
Our paper procurement policy can be found at
www.rbooks.co.uk/environment

Typeset by Palimpsest Book Production Ltd, Grangemouth, Stirlingshire

Printed and bound in Great Britain by
CPI Mackays, Chatham ME5 8TD

CONTENTS

ACKNOWLEDGEMENTS

Grateful acknowledgements are made to the following, in which some of these poems first appeared: *Alhambra Poetry Calendar, Areté, Gallous, The Liberal, Oxford Magazine, Oxford Poetry, Oxford Poetry Broadsides, Poetry Nation Review, Poetry Review, Poetry Wales, The Interpreter's House, The Spectator* and the *Times Literary Supplement.*

'Flotsam' also appeared in a musical sequence, 'A Terrace in Corsica', and was printed in the 2007 Spitalfields Festival programme. 'The Tongue and the Heart' nos 1, 2, 3 and 6 were set by Nicola LeFanu and published under the same title by Peters Edition Ltd. 'Neighbours', 'Reproof', 'The Chair', 'Idling' and 'The Pagoda Revisited' were published as *Five New Poems* (Old World Booklet no. 13) by Old World Books (Venice, 2008). 'Immigrants' was commissioned by the 'Oxford Poets and Refugees Project', a joint initiative of the Oxford Brookes Poetry Centre and Asylum Welcome, and published in *See How I Land* by HeavenTree Press (2009). 'Saint Sebastian' first appeared in *The King's Lynn Silver Folio: poems for Tony Ellis*, ed. Michael Hulse (2009). *The Shell Hymn Book* was published as a pamphlet by the Shoestring Press (2009).

PEBBLE & I

FRAGMENT OF A VICTORIAN DIALOGUE

I asked her: 'Since it is easy to imagine
The unimaginable illnesses
(The bones of the fingers turning into jelly,
Hairs growing in the socket of an eye)
Why is it that we never comprehend
The incomprehensible ones?' She smiled,
Stroking Pebble, her favourite, for its long
Descent into itself and for its utter
Complicity in such a passive process,
Feeling nothing and expecting nothing.
'Because you look for reasons (came the reply)
Of malice, or revenge upon misuse.
Expecting giant rebukes (the confiscation
Of an outraged organ or the disintegration
Of the disputed systems), you do not see
That all is accidental, the result
Of overreaching experiment, of pure
Incompetence. For failure is not a judgement,
It is systemic: the eventual restoration
Of the somatic miracle to common
Matter.' But I, not knowing whether to think
Any matter either common or uncommon,
Given the sport of things existing at all,
Turned to her pale sister who most affected
Me and my kind, feelingly, at the end:
'Why (this was my question) is the event,
The irreversible and final decline,
Accompanied by your severe attention,
Not merely warning, since warnings now were useless,
But painting the withdrawal of your sister
In the cruel colours of a felt collapse?'
And the sister did not smile, but half turned
Away, as if in genuine disappointment.
'Do you not know (she said) that all your pleasure,
All your pain, are all the same, and mine?
They are my gift, in infinite shades within

The body's deep sensorium. Without me
There would be nothing to tell you you exist,
And what I give I cannot take away.'
And so the supreme sisters hand in hand
Went from that place, each with their plaything,
The blithe elder with Pebble, the troubled younger
With the unwilling object of her own
Makeshift, hurtful and unstinting love.
I was not Pebble, and did not want to be.

SEVEN VIALS

She gave me seven vials
Ranked in their colours, bright
As old flags once were.

The first had a dull glow,
Pale as the earliest flowers:
It weighed like a stone in my hand.

The second, a living green,
Seemed to have nowhere to go
But stirred like a leaf in my hand.

The third held a commonplace
Azure of emptiness
And died like hope in my hand.

The fourth was a ripe fruit
Trapped in its purple glass:
It stayed like a bruise on my hand.

The fifth with its stink of death
Laboured to shed its rust
And clung like ice to my hand.

The sixth contained embers
Of a vital distillation
And pulsed like a vein in my hand.

The seventh was the indigo
Of pure questioning
And moved like a hand in my hand.

These were to be poured
In order, and in order
To be for a time preserved.

Spilling and sometimes mixing,
Elements of the eternal
In the ceremony of life.

THREE TIMES

Three times, like wishes or a warning,
It passed him by and made him cry.
First in the morning.

It came to him like sight unseeing,
That closed a door but drew the light
Into his being.

At seven, is a boy to think
Visions will vanish if you stare
Or if you blink?

It passed into him like the shade
Of someone loved he would betray
Or had betrayed.

Nothing was there where it had been,
No chill, no space, nothing precise
That he had seen.

And then at noon, like unfelt touch
That has a power to thrill, though doing
Nothing much.

At thirty, should a man unclasp
A hand he once imagined taking
In his own grasp?

It passed into him like the ghost
Of someone who'd be lost to him
He loved the most.

The shadows lengthen on the court.
The ball was long, the ball was out.
The ball was short.

And now at evening unheard sound
Entered the busy dreaming head
That it had found.

At seventy a man will hear
An echo of all nothings struck
By his own fear.

It passed into him like a bell
That rang for all his losses, and
For him as well.

What were these apparitions but
A trick of the senses to open doors
That they had shut?

Our grief is inward and compelling.
It's ours, and is our fault.
It needs no telling.

SMILES

For Daniel

In the month of your imposing arrival, we found
Some reasons for not being ashamed of the world
We offered you: Lang Lang in his mask of joy
Teasing the rhythms of the Russian master,
And our beaming geraniums (cindery
Kite-tail, jet-and-magenta matelot,
Singed rose). But your own remote response
Was royal and solemn as a Brunswick profile.

For a time, the prompt performances of the body
Are mainly hydraulic. It is the greatest pleasure
To match helplessness with helpfulness,
However often we have performed these tasks.
And we are encouraged by the way you stare at things
(First the front of the watch dangled before you,
Then the back of the watch dangled before you)
Without the benefit of their significance.

Now your head, only lately erect, turning
In order that eyes and ears can equalise
Their twin routes to a source of real interest,
Has acquired its awareness of angle, and something
Of the presence that sculpture likes to celebrate,
That concentration of offered thoughtfulness
In the impassive weight of a bust, the readiness
At last to embody a personality.

And suddenly across the ivory cheeks
Breaks the beautiful expression that
Is all we need to meet your inwardness
With a like gesture, the mirror of greeting.
It pleases not only in being peaceful, this
Broadening of the organ that mostly sucks
And puckers, but in its welcome creation
At last of the ikon of the wholly human.

What fund is it drawn on, your rich signature
Of a smile? And to what if anything does it owe
Its benign response to the attentive family circle
Beyond some aftermath of gratification?
A seal upon calmness of breathing, it says:
Take it as you will, this debt acknowledged,
This fund of pure friendliness, take it gratis,
The first of many mysteries to be mastered.

YAO DEFEN

As I duck my head beneath a playhouse door
I feel myself at once in my grandmother's house
Where I used to think I might be small for ever
And people would lift the heavy tasselled cloth
To peer at me, playing beneath a table,
And smile that unguarded smile of pretended surprise.

Generally we are the size we like to be,
And for a time we are perfectly content
To know more about the underside of drawers
Than bother about the things that are kept inside them,
To listen from little cupboards without real interest
And to squeeze among the lost trophies of attics.

Then to arrive at last at our proper elevation
And to inherit the true scale of our being
Is to find that the world treats us on the level.
No one looks down on us, and hardly up.
There is almost nothing that we are not equal to.
Our height is our relief at being ordinary.

But what do we make of the beautiful poet who
At four-foot six is not the rake he feels?
Or this solemnity on her fortified chair
Who at seven-foot eight is the tallest woman in Asia?
Their lives are miraculous adventures, where
They reach in longing for all that is beyond them.

Ah, but we are all locked into some sadness,
Strangers to our bodies, victims of
Our radiant but unattended smile,
Our welcoming but suffocating embrace,
And their surrender at last in rooms already booked
For them, gratis, at the Hotel Necropole.

THE CHAIR

This is my chair. From which I reach
To feed the logs with the pale blue aura
Of some biscuit foil,
Elusive afterthought,
Flower of a fiery soil.

It is a cradle of supposition,
Receiving me as the stove receives
Its butchered kin,
A fierce intensity
To be consumed within.

And if thought possess its hour of blooming
Between the cooling teapot, say,
Glazed on its trivet
And the golden promise of
A finger of Glenlivet

It is by permission of such treats
That I can blaze with the simple idea
Of a locus where
There is very little to think
But this: this is my chair.

SMALL ROOM IN A HOTEL

In this cool cube of marble
I am valid but invisible
As an image caught in a camera
But not yet reproduced.

My reappearance from confinement
Is that of a lavatory Houdini
Except that no one notices
And the wonder is reduced to a trickle.

How many men have died at stool,
Bent in that vain rictus of hope
That gives to their flushed features
The terrifying squint of a Samurai?

Between philosophical reflections
And the final rebellion of blood
Is the same fine line as between shadows
And the ignorant earth which casts them.

Why are we so eager for shadows?
Is reality so hard to bear?
That our root is in earth which
Returns to earth, and is our sleep?

Each day, wherever we are,
We should rehearse this cancelled debt,
Like a sacrifice whose incense
Ascends into the purity of thought.

ANECDOTE OF AN AMPHIBIOUS AMATEUR

A man is standing on a wave.
His hands appear to be conducting
An invisible orchestra.

The wave is hollowed out in
The colour of old ink bottles.
Tons of it hang in the air.

But time is only at rehearsal.
Faltering, it picks up its pace
And the wave is delivered to the shore.

Where, to the tearing sound of applause,
Its completed chords collapse
Into a dispersal of boiling snow.

And the man? Once nobly erect,
Now folded under, he knows
That the music is larger than he is.

FLOTSAM

Waking on the sea:
As though we have no idea
How we fetched up here

Lifted by a wave
And nudged neither to shore
Nor from it, but stilled

As a calm example of floating,
Contained within movement,
Centre of all dimensions

Like a vast abstraction
In which we might be teased out
By an inquisitive eye.

We have been here for ever
In the afternoon's rehearsal
Of the oblivion of night.

These unlevel lulling litres
Make good claim to be
The true world, or most of it.

Their unresting caress
Is everything we have sought
When yielding to our sleep.

FISH BREAKFAST

Once more into the eight o'clock sea
With stale bread clutched in our fists
And once more over the stones that waves
Wear down to versions of their shapes
That will continue to deceive us,
Proposing that they never change.
The little cup-shapes of the weed
Nodding together in a trance,
These, too, are like each other,
And the shells, without biographies,
Look much the same, like suspects.

Feeding the fish for long enough
Gives hope that we might distinguish them:
That oblade, a hand's length,
Quick to nudge a suspended crust
And sullenly gulping on the turn,
Is there a dawning politics
Of his tribe in the sudden swerving aside
As another's intent surliness
Makes at an angle for the same piece?
Is it an individual weakness
That gives him occasion for resentment?

And those girelles below, feeding
Less greedily on surviving crumbs,
Are they, for instance, at all concerned
By the mystery of provender,
The closeness of the goggled gods?
And further down, the hanging shoal
Of miniature castagonoles,
Unreachable and self-contained
With their poised and scissory tails,
Their blue-black luminosity,
Are they of aloof character?
Can they be said to take a view?

Our cold cradle teaches a lesson:
That pebble, shell, fish, are closer
Than our kind sentiment would have them,
And that we ourselves are quite mad
In our small experience of time
To have assumed a distinctiveness
Above these many material cousins.
It tells us, too, that beauty is only
A function of behaving as things
Are required to behave in their share of years,
And even we are beautiful.

THE LOVE THREAD

Two little love birds fly in and out
Of the arching sarsaparilla hedge,
Neither greeting nor ignoring the other.
This is what they do, no notion
Of self-performance, no sense of habit.
For them, purpose lies in the doing:
The breasting of the wind, the falling back,
The spooling of an invisible thread
Of fluttering and separation
Before they cross again, like a tied
Bow, over and over and over.
This is their annual wooing in the blue
Above the trowel-leaves of the hedge,
And in the hedge, where life breeds.
But now they have nested in a basket
Hanging above the shed for old shoes
And lobster-pots, as if chancing
A brave familiarity
With the nude lords of their demesne,
Though Ange says they have abandoned it
Now that the summer makes things busy.
So there is nothing more to say.

IDLING

Living in the present as a mere participle,
When nothing much moves but the slow
Shade of the parasol like a sundial,
Is to forget how it all began,
Imperative and conditional,
With no thought of what it might one day feel like:
The lost luggage of an existence already passed,
All written up, like a claim on insurance.

To indulge like this seems a folly,
But in that time of rueful reckonings,
Nerved to take account of where I might have arrived
And what I shall have achieved,
I reckon I may at least be future perfect.

THE PAGODA REVISITED

Chanteloup, Amboise

This monument to a view of nothing
(Its abolished château) has every reason
To admire itself for its persistence.
At the end of a peaceable gravel drive
Among well-watered swans, its tiers
Provide a circular ascent in stages
Like the ages of man. But here we are at the
Top suddenly, aware of the crumbling stone
And iron reinforcement of the loose rails.
It is as narrow as being in your own head,
And you can think of nothing but getting down.

THE SWALLOWS AT CHENONCEAU

'S'il vient à point, me souviendra.' Thomas Bohier

Their building is never finished
Nor their life in the blue air.

Their looping trajectories
Capture invisibility

And return with easy accuracy
To breeding slits and crannies

Clustered beneath the eyebrows
Of these long-suffering turrets

Stone bleached by the sun,
Capped by tented slate.

A tail is seen just for a moment
Before disappearing inside.

No intrigue as patent
In such eager soaring and hovering

Nothing so guileless,
Nothing so anonymous

No calmness nor order of gardens
Could redeem this profusion

Nor effort of history,
Nor stone's severity.

Memory not conditional,
But continual.

THE SHELL HYMN BOOK

1 *A Hard Thing to Sell*

Never at rest
Once it has started,
Our heart's tender-hearted
In its medals of chest.

Our kidneys and liver
Lie fairly protected
By ribs well-connected,
But the blood like a river

Flows over the bone
And the skin grows outside
In an effort to hide
What shouldn't be shown:

Our jingly skeleton
(Od's-bodikins!)
All knuckles and shins
Like the Duke of Wellington.

We speak with our faces
And can wrinkle our noses
And loll in soft poses
Or the idlest embraces

But in life's decrescendo
If it seems second-best
As a way to be dressed,
Not exo- but endo-

And our flesh seems a thing
That a simple machete
Can turn to spaghetti,
And we feel every sting,

Think: a crab's never naked,
Making love in full armour

Of shelly pyjama.
It's a hard way to make it.

It's a hard way to live.
It's a hard thing to sell
Is life in a shell.
It's hard to forgive.

But in God's weird endeavour
It's outside or inside,
Boneside or skinside,
So give thanks to whichever.

Give thanks to your skin!
Give thanks to your shell!
And move heaven and hell
To remain therein.

2 *The Trumpet Addresses the Limpet*

The trumpet warns of war's alarms
With arguments beyond persuasion.
Now must the limpet take up arms
   Against invasion.

Well-tuned, the trumpet stops its noise.
Alternate fingers smooth the salve
(The artless limpet still employs
   A single valve).

The trumpet speaks the glare of empire.
The limpet from its hiding-place
Has learned for years to keep its temper,
   All foot, no face.

The trumpet blows an ancient story,
The tramp of trespass without end.
The limpet has no territory
   It can defend.

This horny nipple on its base
Of rock's so slow as to be static,

Secure within its pointy space
　　Like an attic.

It hoards delusions of the sea
That everything is what it seems.
Washed in that cold immensity
　　It dreams and dreams.

But surely it will come to pass
That some grim grandma will arrive
To tear it off, as bold as brass,
　　Eat it alive.

Ripped from its rock in cruel abruption
In valediction valvular,
This final fatal interruption
　　Will leave no scar.

The creature is transmogrified
And briefly nude, its aureole
Resplendent as it's popped inside
　　And swallowed whole.

What greed esteems is got by stealth.
No creature lives entirely free,
Even in that broad commonwealth
　　The unfenced sea.

This is their Eden's irksome crinkle
That to the happy prawn and shrimp it
Falls to die. Also the winkle
　　And the limpet.

They die, whether they live in swarms
Or are determined solipsists.
Whatever their multivarious forms,
　　Harsh fate insists.

And thus the trumpet, after all,
Delivers to the uttermost

Its limpid democratic call,
    The Last Post.

To you and me not least it sounds,
Though our foundations feel secure:
The daze of Love, the pleasure-grounds
    Of Literature.

Each in our shelly wigwam hides,
Fast in our purpose, though contentious;
Daily are nourished by the tides
    That duly drench us.

Our one illusion is a sport,
That what we gain will somehow last,
Our little empire a mere thought
    Of what has passed.

3 Neither One Thing Nor the Other

A man of sanguine temperament
    Came to a barren shore,
And there his sanguine days were spent
    Each like the one before.

The shore, the shore, the barren shore!
    Not fisherman, nor farmer,
Caught in between, he sought therefore
    To supplicate his karma.

No squid to spit, no lamb to carve,
    He lived a bleak existence.
Likely enough that he would starve.
    He needed some assistance.

His karma said, as karmas do,
    'The choice was bad, and yours.'
And he replied: 'That may be true,
    But please be my Santa Claus.'

His karma looked again and said:
    'Indeed, I see thou starvest.

The sea is fish, the land is bread,
    But here there is no harvest.'

'A harvest, though, is what I need.
    I know I've been a fool.'
'You have. But still, you've got to feed.
    Look in that rocky pool.'

And there he found a mussel-bed
    And straight away waxed lyrical:
'I have no fish, I have no bread,
    But here I have a miracle!

'Food in the form of salty flesh
    In shelly chariots,
Immobile, plentiful and fresh,
    The black of ancient pots.

'Open to suck the stilly shallows,
    Closed to the probing touch,
Half feels like grit, half like marshmallow,
    And tastes of nothing much.'

The moral of this doubtful tale?
    It's easy to be trusting:
A feast is just a fingernail
    From something quite disgusting.

And there's an art in eating mussels:
    Your karma's incomplete
Until you've sat in golden Brussels
    And eaten *moules et frites*.

4 *The Lobster Gets a Grip*

    As chobdars obdurate in
    Their noble masters' cause
    Take besoms of bright straws
    In the prompt discipline
Of sweeping from the public street
Urchins assembling at their feet

So the lobster keeps
The sea bed clear before him:
The creatures can't ignore him,
But lurch in panic heaps
Before the silent Fee-Faw-Fum
Of his serrated bulldog thumb.

The bobstay stays the ship
  In stormy weather.
The gobstop stops your gob
  Altogether.
The stopgap does its job
  But not for ever.
And the lobster gets a grip:
  First prize for endeavour.

Were our whole appearance
  To assume so obviously
The role of weapon, to be
  Both warning and defence,
We might, with cautious statesmanship,
Become accustomed to its grip.

And yet, to scuttle through
  The weeds, irresolute,
Extending a salute
  At all encounters: who
Would not feel that baleful forfex
A brute display of chelamorphics?

The sobster *con amore*
Preys on each listening friend.
The jobster's hour of glory
Lies in a dividend.
The mobster growls: 'Signore,
You do not comprehend!'
But the lobster's little story
Lies in its gripping end.

5 Turning Turtle

*'Have your callapash or deep shell done round the edges with paste,
season it in the inside with Cayenne pepper and salt, and a little
Madeira wine, bake it half an hour, then put in the lungs and
white meat, force-meat, and eggs over, and bake it half an hour . . .
Take the callapee, run your knife between the meat and shell, and
fill it full of force-meat; season it all over with sweet herbs chopped
fine, a shallot chopped, Cayenne pepper and salt, and a little
Madeira wine; put a paste round the edge, and bake it an hour and
a half.'* Mrs Glasse

The turtle knows she must go smash
When spied by those who sail upon
The liquid roof of her abode
   Calipee! Calipash!
Who with their skilled brutality
Bring Carib treats to Albion
Along the slavers' dipping road
   Calipash! Calipee!

A ragged crew, whose sabres flash
On harvest of the nets released,
The one-eyed and the timber-toed
   Calipee! Calipash!
Fortune has blessed the gluttony
That fetches turtles for a feast,
Pardons each lustful episode
   Calipash! Calipee!

Like the dragoon who makes his dash,
The turtle knows the right direction
In which to turn her carapace
   Calipee! Calipash!
And her surrender lets us see
That flight can be some brief protection
From the exhaustion of the chase
   Calipash! Calipee!

In eager dreams, with great panache
She meets at last her nemesis.
Turning, she finds no hiding-place
    Calipee! Calipash!
Always this ambiguity:
Capsized, she knows that cowardice
Has means to make a braver face
    Calipash! Calipee!

The turtle's the opposite of rash,
Like saints obedient to burn
In fire that fatally refines them
    Calipee! Calipash!
She thinks to meet her enemy
As lovers in submission turn
From the great longing that defines them
    Calipash! Calipee!

This pliancy betrays a clash
Of motives in the mad pursuit
That both excites and undermines them
    Calipash! Calipee!
Their star in its immensity
Inspires them, though irresolute;
Though dazzled and betrayed, outshines them
    Calipash! Calipee!

6 Festin d'Oursin

Lunch is walking across my plate,
Not for long, but long enough.
My spoon descends. It is too late.
I call the moving creature's bluff.
A squeeze of quartered lemon begs
Forgiveness of the stirring legs.

Christian tore them from their rocks
With an adept unfeeling glove
And put them in a floating box.
We know there is no better love

Than of this naked beast who dines
On such fine ovoids wigged with spines.

He wields the scissored guillotine
To split the needled cranium wide:
The orange that is almost green
Lies like the five splayed wounds inside,
The body (as the prophet saith)
Crossed in the compass points of death.

For God is great who made the sea
A scene for such a sacrifice.
Its natural fecundity
Exacts an elementary price,
And he is merciful to send
His creatures to their proper end.

In life, the little sea-bears wait
In patience for their passing prey,
While we must venture out to bait
The swarming shallows of the bay.
Thus are we priestly when we dine,
And break the bread, and pour the wine.

Noon is a living sacrament,
A banquet of the suffering flesh,
A blessing in the spoon's descent,
A strange redemption of the *pêche*
Where souls are gathered and are spilled
Upon the plate to prove our guilt.

GALLERY

Of the various gods we take for granted
Of which we may take our museum choice,
By none of them are we nightly haunted,
From none devise a daily voice.

The hero steps back into his story.
His miracles have been unmasked,
Adventures merely allegory
Whose meaning may not now be asked.

Even majestic images
We long to give a second look
Can be explained in prose that is
As cool and closed as any book.

The god whose sharpened teeth are gems
To make devouring more delicious.
The god who equally condemns
Those who are virtuous and vicious.

The god with firebolts in his fist
Looking for men to pile them on,
A zoomorphic amorist
Equally bold as bull or swan.

The god, erect, dispelling fear,
With that small inward smile you see
On curates only half-sincere
In turning down a cup of tea.

And then the bearded one who stood
Silent amid an angry crowd,
Shouldering his death in wood
Winged like a windmill in a cloud.

No nearer now to any myth,
Remote from any ritual,
The altar or the monolith,
Our disbeliefs habitual.

From room to room, from wall to wall
We wander through the centuries
Appraising and admiring all.
Our life alone is ours to please.

PROGRÈS DE SA MAJESTÉ LE SOLEIL

Nor shall he ever be induced
To manifest himself to us
And condescend, as he was used
To do, to his petitioners.

To leave the gold arch of his gladness
And turn to us in recognition,
As Bacchus once of Ariadne's
Grief, in those draperies of Titian.

How could we interrupt the course
Of that mysterious procession,
Demanding, with a puny force,
One final, saving intercession?

There would be laughter in the skies
At such presumption in our schemes;
A general sadness, too; surprise
At our hopes and our outrageous dreams.

On, on! His sweeping robe
Defines the dwindling of the light
Beyond the ever-cooling globe
And the great chasms of the night.

One god left, and one god only,
Mortal now, as all gods are
Who ever loved us, conscious and lonely
Beneath our doomed and singular star.

OUT

Good morning, Vicar! How's your rhubarb?
What's happened to your team's catholicon?
How will you play the game with both hips gone?
Or take your Tio Pepe from Miss Sweetbird
    Without a stain on her cretonne?

You played a straight bat in your second innings.
You made a straight bet on the human race.
Your gravitas is gravy on your face
And it's not over. Do not collect your winnings.
    Throw again, and pass the dice.

You tore the stub from our expensive ticket
And thought to welcome us upon your cloud,
But don't you know your turn's been disallowed?
Can't you see the scattered bits of wicket?
    And hear the hooting of the crowd?

And now you stalk back to the dark pavilion
With all your strokes unplayable and your
Sour chin held high like an ambassador
Dismissed by a committee: thanks a million!
    Now we, and you, all know the score.

REPROOF

How often we say: 'I've only myself
To blame' when we'd really like to say
'There's no one who cares enough to blame us.'

Those times when we could see it coming,
Whatever it was, and knew that we needed
Both the confirmation and the reproof.

Without warning, you are alone.
You are your own authority.
You've only yourself to do the blaming.

That wagging lifted finger is a cartoon
Of all that is absent from your eager life,
Suspended in a thought-bubble above your head.

The plaster mould lies in pieces at your feet.
You have become your own horizon of foreboding,
And the sky shrinks to the surface of the skin.

TIME

Where are the blue-black castagonoles of yester?
Or Proust the owl, glimmering from his pole?
Pigeons are nesting in your pigeon-hole.
What is John Jarndyce doing without Esther?
And what do we think became of poor Sir Leicester?

Ripe on the hour, the hidden carcinoma
Unveils the life that it can never be.
Summer's last figs are gathered from the tree:
You sit all morning in their frail aroma.
The orange lily sinks into a coma.

On the horizon, the sails like unread pages
Will still be there when you no longer see them.
Moths that go nowhere quickly when you free them
Burst into flames. The pebbles last for ages.
Earth's many seas are restless in their cages.

Now stone that burns is quite another matter.
It shows you how eternity is reckoned.
For everything is drawn into that second
When the eye strikes and the bright stars scatter.
The former lasts no longer than the latter.

GUARANTEES

We fear machines just as we fear
Our bodies, when they begin to fail.
The parallels are demoralising.

A raw thud and judder, a helpless
Clatter, or worse, a silent refusal,
The small green light gone out.

There was a once when, if we cared to,
We understood the way things worked
And happily drove ourselves to death.

Now, sadly, the position has
Reversed: we are obsessed by what
We know of our precarious health

But careless of the mystery
We expensive working creatures have
Become, beyond our guarantees.

NEIGHBOURS

Noises in the night, occasional
Requests, odd or offensive habits:
We know only enough about them

To place them on a scale of threat,
Of comedy, or likely boredom.
Their faces are as familiar as shrubs.

Letters to be redirected
Are windows into their hidden lives,
Or ten empty Bells beside the bin,

A suddenly noticed absence, a ramping
Lawn, the blue pulse of an ambulance:
Their lives' climax could be ours.

IMMIGRANTS

1 Babies

We've no idea how odd we look. But surely
That will endear us to our enemies
(Our hosts, we mean) who judge us prematurely
For all the things about us that don't please?
They have the prejudice of prior existence.
They are the tall ones, lords of the ancient earth.
The only weapon in our weak resistance
Is the half-intended accident of birth.

History the Punisher can't say
A lot about the future, good intentions,
Or the irrelevant charm of our pretensions.
But no one tells us we must go away
And our unsettling is far more commonplace,
Since we are immigrants in time, not place.

2 Languages

Who taught us the geography of blood?
Who can retrieve the speech of Paradise?
The jokes of Noah's sons before the Flood?
The names for hunger in an age of ice?
Who killed his brother for a shibboleth?
Who discovered fear? Who started fires
In countries other than his own? Whose death
Became a football field between the wires?

The human story is a long dispersal.
Our babble is a weapon in our hands
That we're embarrassed by, a universal
Accident of brief connecting strands
That strain and twist, abrasive as a rope
That binds us to our shame, and to our hope.

3 Here

Here is the where of all belonging, light
Of all our self-created lives. The whence
Of limitations pointed (at the height
Of their long century's cruel confidence)
To what my great-grandparents came to see
As a tantalising future, theirs by right
And something different they could choose to be,
Ditching their class or county overnight.

The history of every family
Pivots upon some moment when a move
Is made: some minor struggle to be free,
Some little stubbornness, something to prove,
Oppression or frustration, boredom or fear,
When we would rather not be there, but here.

4 Choices

Here, said Minnie, in her Fulham terrace,
Bearing the children of her furrier.
(Since no policeman's daughter is an heiress,
Seeking a fortune must be up to her.)
Here, said Lister, heart fluttering like a mouse,
In ill-health laying down his tools to pay
For a spanking brand-new Blackpool boarding-house.
(A blacksmith has a right to be a rentier.)

Where can we find ourselves but in our being
Exactly what we know we need to be?
That's how the human enterprise survives.
How much more necessary, then, when fleeing
The world's injustice, in terror of our lives,
That we be welcome anywhere. And free.

NEWSPAPERS

Good morning to the happy world.
Someone comes whistling round a corner
And his house is still there.

Is this so surprising? Are we
To hang by our thumbs? Our children served
To us on spits?

The newspapers remind us daily
That accident, coincidence and surprise
Are rare and remarkable.

But we know too much for our own good,
More than we should. We can't unknow
The worst that we know.

The pianist's fingers stamped to a pulp,
The baby raped while still attached
By the cord to the mother.

And our own droll deficiencies,
Criticising a soapy vermouth
Or dreaming of fame

While devout ministers are practising war
And the earth's bounty is priced beyond
The purse of the million.

What we fear the most is always
Still to happen, and may not.
But that is theory.

We are resigned to living by the customs
That won't outrage or disappoint us.
Is that philosophy?

In the real world something is always
Happening, and happening to someone.
We hope not us.

CARD HOUSES

The air was angry all the night,
Drum-rolling on the dormer
And bottle-blowing the chimney.

I thought maybe that the mountain
Was taking revenge on the roof
For the stealing of slate.

The day that the deck was dealt
Out to the village, violence
Was proposed to its profile.

The scope of the sky was altered.
Stone was split and stacked,
Transported, and nailed to timbers.

Houses deserve to be dry,
But a hill needs a level head
Not to quarrel with a quarry.

The wind is a reminder of wrath,
A momentary mineral alliance,
The dunning of a debt.

Its fingers grip the gutters,
Twisting and tugging at the eaves.
The roof comes loose like a lid.

And vaults all over the valley,
Slates flapping their feathers,
Blue-black as ravens.

Slates stream like a causeway,
A conjuror's spurted shuffle
Frittering over the fields.

So I thought, deep in our duvet,
Listening to the lost leaves
And the thrashing of the ash tree.

But it was only my heart's hammering
And fear of the frailness of houses,
Only my silly sleeplessness

That spoke to me of spooks
And warned of walls and windows
Left standing in shapes of stone

Trembling to tumble inwards
At the barest of breaths,
One after the other.

In the shadowing sun of the morning
The mountain was itself once more,
Looking calm enough in its keep.

It wore the appearance of apex
In that vague violet of a grey
That has endured epochs.

And there was no hint of harm:
Songbirds settling on the slates
Reckoned them as good as rock

And the angles argued respect
For their share of local shape
In every particular point.

Since the world hosts our happiness
It is only proper to presume
That there is mountain enough for men.

It has endured erosion,
And appears altogether
Calm about collapsing.

In any case, we conclude
That the future will have forgotten
Our naturally tumbling towers

And what we dare in our depredations
Is nothing like the nemesis
That time idly toys with.

HENDRE FAWR

We plod on the brow of the-field-with-the-stone,
That contour between level passivity
And an offering tilt that greets the sun,
And we expect in the course of things to find
Mushrooms, because indeed they grow there.
They are in their appearances neither shy nor brazen,
Taking their time to shoulder up, one by one,
And looking surprised to find others nearby
Who have, like them, come to as much
Of a corner in the grass as they could find
To show themselves and become companions.

We conclude that we are like them, but in motion,
Circling in a planetary complication
About our idea of some future discovery,
You walking up with an inquisitive stoop,
I in a careless saunter, kicking at thistles.
But we know that the future is only lying in wait
And as little to be trusted as anything unknown.
We have lost the expectation of the ordinary miracle
In the iron prow and sweeping arm of the farmer
Whose watching of weather is a working practice
And the act of ambulation a care of the bounds.

What has already happened was sometimes marvellous,
Like Rowland coming across the grass to us,
Bringing his new neighbours mushrooms in spread hands,
Their cups the sizeable size of his own cap,
The yield of them as complete as his smile,
And the smell (fern-root, aniseed, leaf-mould,
A whiff of kidney) telling of the ancient ways of the field,
A place that horses once would amble from and pause
And lift their heads and briefly snort, grown old
From bracing shoulders against the long drag of the land,
Yearning down the valley to the barking farm.

GOLF BALL WALK

Porth Dinllaen

On this spit of turf, cradled
Above unshaveable falls
Of tumbling granite

Golfers discuss the lengthen-
ing and shortening at once
Of their shots and odds.

Pulling weapons behind them
Like travellers in their great
Concourse of empire.

And we, avoiding alike
The sacred greens and vistas
Of their mystery

Tread the boundary of the
Reserved circuits regardless
Of the privilege

And of the ironsprung thlock
And blind careless whistling of
Their dimpled missiles

(A drive too wide could give you
An incurable headache,
Singled out by fate

And the peace of the morning
To be the chance victim of
A ludic sniping),

Taking the precaution of
Revenge, collecting golf balls
From the springy rough:

Poking in neglected grass,
Just the boot's toe is enough,
Nudging a tussock.

On either side of the course
The sea swirls and gollops the rocks
Where seals stretch their necks

Or edge and shuffle into
Its relaxing element
Where they become waves

Of darker colour, twisting
Beneath its restless surface
In pursuit of fish.

Sometimes, replete, their faces
Appear above the water,
Surprisingly calm,

Affecting an unconcern
Like a diner looking round
For the wine waiter.

The nature of our free choice
To be there and to observe
Such things is itself

A topic for quiet thought
As we circumambulate
The perimeter.

Other things are displaying
The readiness to be what
They are when required:

Red and orange lobster-floats
Like balloons escaping from
A ceiling of sea.

The lifeboat in its stone box
Like a giant's unwrapped toy,
Bright brass, and cream paint.

Rope coiled round and round itself
Like liquorice, and damp nets
Half-tidied away.

The first wisps of a late fire
From the chimney of Ty Goch,
A childish scribble

Quietly announcing its
Cure for loneliness and thirst
To passing pilgrims,

An ascending smoke of bells
From the little sandlocked inn
Where cold gulls keep guard.

And yes, we fully intend
To join that congregation,
Its foaming amber.

It will complete the morning,
The closing of a circle,
A knot, a flourish.

And yet, like everything
Imagined within the mind,
It is still to come.

Heading into the pale sun,
We pause on a slight incline,
Hearing something new:

The furious jabber of
A skylark snagged on the air,
Struggling to get free.

It's up there at the top of
Its invisible ladder,
High enough to see

If it wanted to, both sides
Of the thin promontory
And its distinct shores.

Whatever its perspective
Delivers in the leisure
Needed to know it

(Surely nothing to do with
Fly-catching or attracting
Another skylark)

It is a fine feat of sight
And an unusual height
Worth singing about.

It must see more than we do,
Though what it can make of it
Is entirely doubtful.

And in any case, our own
Pleasure lies in taking things
Simply as they come.

One following the other,
Not always predictable,
Although recognised.

Intermittently we see
Something of where we came from
And the path ahead.

We find ourselves at a point
Where familiarity
Is no delusion

And what we have seen before
And what we said about it
Has become sacred

Like this roundabout walk
And its perfectly arranged
Length and scenery:

The flags in sequence, the seals,
The crucified cormorants,
The nested golf-balls,

The expected arrival,
The view in front of us of
What was once behind.

Our life will never link up
With itself. It goes on, and
Has no returning.

It goes on, just for a time,
And when it stops there is no
Turning back at all.

PLATFORM

The stillness of this mountain halt,
Rails curving in the sun around
The bend into a dark wood,
Is like surprising in oneself
An insight into the possible.

To walk up here, to find by chance
A steel intention palpable
Among these ancient oaks, with slate
And rhododendrons collapsed and sprawling,
Is to stumble upon a wonder.

The wooden platform is no more
Than a stand to raise you from the nettles
And filleted bones of fern that crowd it.
You might stare in each direction for hours
And at your wristwatch with impatience.

To deliver speeches while you wait
Would be a natural consequence
Of the mild and philosophical
Excitement in which you find yourself,
But there is no one who would hear you.

Except the inconsequential birds
Shitting berries in a clearing,
Who call only to each other
And listen only for like sounds
That have some likely meaning for them.

It is a museum of lost journeys,
The suspended survival of a decision
To join two useful distances
By the latest means. At either end
The purpose has been long forgotten.

Your footsteps lightly creak upon
This pulpit of the afternoon.
The moment is one of all too few
Within the strange parentheses
Of your own origin and end.

KOSHKA

1

Sometimes you came to ask a question:
That silent arresting look of yours,
A lift of the head, the kneading of paws,
   The slowest of slow blinks
And a pretence of unconcern.
   You will not ask it now.

Empty, the places where you sat:
The window's vantage, or the edge
Of wall, or disregarded ledge
   Where you could face your foes,
A yellow carpet patch of sun.
   You will not sit there now.

Your movements noticed here and there,
Your steady ruminating walk
From room to room, that ambling stalk
   As if in quest of something
Partly assembled in your mind.
   You will not go there now.

Your eyes were the liquid mirrors of distance
When all the things we couldn't see
Became for you the two or three
   Significant images
That gave your leaping body purpose.
   You will not see them now.

In age, your head would sometimes droop
When sitting quietly in a doze,
And lift again, as if the nose
   Took up its sentry post,
Prompted by some delicious dream.
   You will not lift it now.

Where you are is the nowhere that we fear,
The spaceless unappetising future, the past
Before memory, the present without being.
You did not know it was about to happen,
Lost in my cradling arm, the lightness of a doll
Whose head, empty of life, dropped back.

That was our knowledge, ours the final vigil
Once the fatal arrangements had been made.
The knowledge is our pain, also our gift
That lets me write these lines in celebration
Of a small blue cat, nervous of disposition
But friendly and attentive when so inclined.

It is an unwelcome gift, hateful to think it.
Knowing how soon the secret sluices of the body
Rust in their ratchets, how the glistening glands
Dry to a throb of stone and pause in their pulse,
Is to know a truth as fixed as a date on a coin
Thoughtlessly hoarded, that is still to spend.

For it is our death that we somehow mourn
In yours, still pacing the enchanting towers
And terraces where we must waste our days,
And this is our own life to be spilled out through
Our hooped reluctant arms, as though releasing
A cat aching and eager to be away.

DARTINGTON REVISITED

For Daniel

I'm off to Willi Soukop's donkey
In the little place where he waits for me.
There in the space beneath the trees
Where the lawn declines and disappears,
Where over the mown roots and fallen
Mulberries and all in a merry catch
Her practised nymphs are singing
Their ringing praises of Diana
Outside a summer-house of thatch,
There he waits for me.

Tiny birds are flying level into the hanging
Cedars where their recitatives
Declare it is summer again.
By the gravel path, under the broad leaves,
There is light laughter among the ranks
Of the admiring spectators.
His flanks are dewy with his long waiting.
His hooves are deep in stone.
My arms are round his neck at the starting-gate,
My lips on the chill bronze,
Him and me alone, throughout
The long summer.

PIANO MASTERCLASS

For Rolf Hind

1

The piano is opened
And lifts a hopeful wing.

Phrases are to be freed
From their locked pace

From the weather of flat fingers
And the impositions of posture.

Scriabin unscrambled
From code to cadence

From half-vision
To the visionary.

2

It sits forward on its knuckles
Glossy as a gorilla.

Its bared teeth
Are neither a smile nor a snarl.

Beneath its raised eyebrows
A swarm of mixed signals

Which must be confronted
With a patient stroking.

Its great roaring
Is an eventual liberation.

3

The feckless prelude,
The necklace unpearled

And now to be restrung,
The picture rehung

The proportions restored
And the fingers grateful

For their sudden release
And disappearance up the ladder

Like a cloud of peace,
Like a flight of angels.

4

Debussy's poorly piano
Is making good progress.

Delicate exercises,
Pressing and pointing.

The first cautious steps
Of a spacious dance.

The renewed stamina,
The unlooked-for elation.

The plurality of notes,
The singularity of idea.

5

Brahms in slow-motion,
All arms and fists.

The thunder is broken
Into clumsy pieces

Peering into the notes
As into a middle distance

Or the eye of a storm
That will whirl us away

One day, one day,
The hands perfectly full.

SHELLS

Sun brings out the dazzle on this
Glittering stretch of lonely beach.
Treading on the sizeable sand
You find that its dry creaking bulk
Is a bright random assemblage
Of large grains and very small shells,
Each of the latter the dead hulk
Of some lost watery comma,
A once-determined sea-creature
Who for a paltry length of time
Added its voice to the sea's rage.

In your hand they tell of marvels
Performed on these warm granite coasts:
The orange-and-tan fan smaller
Than a child's little fingernail,
The teardrop whelk, the snail's spiral
Green like a tennis eyeshade and
Hardly bigger than a match head.
This display turns us into gods
Proceeding to our vain pleasures
Across billions of jewels
That were sea-houses, and their ghosts.

THE JETSAM GARDEN

For Felix

On a reach of sun-baked pebbles near the tide-line
Where the stumbling beach lifts slightly like the fine
Barely-shifting gradient of a recumbent body,
Lodged in that untrudged no-man's-land between
The groin of the swirling rocks and the tousled headland

The garden is still visible in its surprising extent
As an unusual enclave of perpendicular shapes,
Like a city seen from a jet on its final descent
Or a placement of toys left out on a carpet
Whose pattern itself had prompted their arrangement.

Blind eyes staring from their igneous mass,
The pebbles wear only the chalky shadow
Of the colours that the sea drenches them in
As it picks them up and slowly turns them
Over in the season of its distress, like problems.

They nudge now in little mounds and lines,
And stuck among them are the dried sprays of fir,
Straws, twigs and plastic ice-cream spines
(White, cerise, magenta, vermilion)
That constitute the garden's vegetation.

Some stones serve as pedestals in places
For fragile figures in their avenues:
Sea urchins, salt-whitened screw-caps, driftweed,
Aquiline half-pegs with blue string arms, surround
The heroes of extemporised civic spaces.

A half-inch cowboy hat in silent cheers
Twirls on a leaning tower of split bamboo.
Another flies a fan of feathers bound
With greenish wire, crusty and oxidised,
Above a mosaic face, cork nose, shell ears.

And charcoal legends elevated there
Look on benignly at the plinths and towers.
There are proprietary names, and a sign
That points in the one direction that it would
Ever occur to it to point: 'La Mer'.

You appraised it, as an architect might do,
With the lordly detachment of a limpet monocle.
You returned with the helpful delivery of new
And unlikely materials ('Here we go!')
And the patient splitting and twiddling of their parts.

And now a week has passed, and you are gone.
The garden hears nothing but the tranquil sea.
Absence is not only a necessary absenting,
When we imagine an elsewhere entered upon
Like a new chapter in an exciting story.

It is also, and much more, a palpable ache
That refuses every hope and compensation.
It is the loneliness of the places that we make,
Like the little garden without you, lost in itself
And in the blankness of nothing to do, or to be done.

LIBECCIO

The orange petals lift in the libeccio
Like the shoulders of girls being kissed upon the neck.
It shifts the random spillage along the terrace
(Breadcrumbs, grape-pips, toenails, pistachio-shells)
Like a gambler counting his chips to the table edge
And letting them drop into a practised palm.
It blows across the rapt profile of siesta,
Legs tucked up on the day-bed, the hand on the cheek,
And the mind exploring in wonder its gift from the bottle.
The hanging strips of the terrace curtain stir,
Cream/chocolate/amber/chocolate/cream,
With a distant whisper of insistent gossip,
And the sea begins to tear itself to pieces.

We have shut ourselves from these continuous sounds
As having no urgent claim on our peaceful dreams.
But perhaps we should take note of its querulous meddling,
This warm wind whose ambition is to be spent
Here and now at our centre of consciousness.
It blows with a sense of its belated longing,
Like an old man in the sudden fullness of memory,
Salacious, wistful, destructive, impotent.

TELL ME

Dilla ancora
La parola che consola . . .
Dilla ancora! Tosca

So when the page is turned and the breath is stilled
And there are no sustaining vows or voices
And our blood stops in the half-second that
Leaves unsolved its ancient paradox
(Earth to earth? A fluttering at the gates?)
We have become the story of our life
And there is nothing more to say.

Though there be torture in the second act
Or deadly error in the third, we were
Duly briefed by the many legends.
We adopted banners for fresh exploit
And held our future for a moment in our arms.

We think it worth it, whatever it cost.
We turn down the corner of that final page
And nod wisely, and sing into the air:
'For this, anything ever thought or written
Were but a vain parley, a challenge in the wind.
For this we risked everything. Judge us so.'
But nothing is heard of that. It has all passed.

NATURA MORTA BY GIORGIO MORANDI

For Saul

This moving world, alive before our eyes
Like a bold narrative of its own life,
Assumes a point of view where nothing dies.

October trees in drizzle, taxis stopping
Before the bright banners of the galleries
Where tourists pause a moment with their shopping.

But inside nothing stops, or starts, or pauses.
The paintings reach in stillness for the hand
That put them there, locked in their first causes.

Flagons, bottles, boxes, cups: a frieze
As close as may be to that purity
Which has no restless consequence to please.

And you, Morandi, in a bleak elation
Of the abstracted spirit, calmly propose
Your metaphysics of refiguration.

'Only we can know a cup's a cup,'
You say. But so we do. And what is left,
However bitter, we must drink it up.

Again and again your shapes assume their places,
As if familiarity could help
Us to convert their nature into stasis.

Think of the Dutch, who valued appetite.
A carp or tulip was the thing itself,
Albeit conjured by their tricks of light.

Their world's unarguably one we know,
The garden where our contemplation blooms,
The kitchen borrowed by the studio.

Their sensuous uses occupy our thoughts.
In the midnight foyer of the Dream Hotel,
Fish that seem dead are simply out of sorts.

If nature must be dead, as nature will
And all too soon, then let us not despair.
Still we are poets of life, and keeping still.

SAINT SEBASTIAN

By Raffaello Sanzio, in Bergamo

For Tony Ellis, in King's Lynn

This is what the arrow sings:
So many feathers, never wings.

Between the finger and the thumb
He holds the arrow's weighted shaft
As though the promised martyrdom
Took nothing but a painter's craft
To choose the pigments he must crush,
The mortar he must mix them in,
And delicately lift a brush
To pierce the beauty of the skin.

This is what the arrow sings:
So many feathers, never wings.

The bright hem of his shirt engraves,
Like a crow's footprints in the snow,
Stitches of minims on their staves
That show the arrows where to go.
The saint's a mirror of the soul
That basks in this Italian air
Beneath the sun's bright aureole
And looks to be translated there.

This is what the arrow sings:
So many feathers, never wings.

His tunic's brush-strokes decorate
The soft anatomy they hide
With flowers multifoliate.
A heart is pumping blood inside,
And loosened arrows, swift and glib,
Will write upon the linen's mesh

With furious hagiographic nib
Their model of the word made *flèche*.

This is what the arrow sings:
So many feathers, never wings.

PAESTUM

For Peter Porter at eighty

Yesterday the sinuous Amalfi coast,
With its netted lemons the size of babies' heads;
Today a bleaker stretch towards the south,
An outpost of eleventh-century Byzantium
Where a poet's hunger for eternity
Can be fairly matched by the philosopher's
Nostalgia for the accidence of birth.
The place was named for Poseidon, shape-changer,
Greedy for the bodies of boys, and is the site
Of fluted temples devoted to appeasement
Of the sea's fury and its impermanence.
We could both, couldn't we, easily visualise
That English poet who idly wandered here
In his ambition and his amorous exile?

On seeded ruins licked by scuttling lizards
(Who for a moment pause, their pale blue throats
Pulsing with life beneath their chequered green
And black) he himself in his lizardly pleasure
Paused, waistcoat unbuttoned to the sun,
To admire the mountains through the open roof
Of Neptune's temple, broken to the clouds.
At such a moment, verse is one response
To earnest glimpses of the infinite,
And ignorance the best excuse of youth.
The sea would have him soon, yawning over
His jaunty yacht, plucking with sated relish
The sodden legs, and hair, and the clutched hat,
The mountains declining his Promethean myth.

But the philosopher, for whom a glass among friends
Was the right response to an intuition of death
And who embraced it willingly in his high
Symbolic dive into that element
Which is for ever and ever changing shape,

Had long ago made his loving farewells
To talk, companionship, the search for truth;
Long ago had settled his account
With the irrelevant temples and all the little
Uncompleted tasks that filled his day;
Long ago had said good-bye to longing,
And to the sun, and to the lizard-shadowed stone,
Tucked in his head, and put his hands together
In the gesture that is both prow and prayer – and plunged.

STOP

Terra Nostra di Salamone Filippo e Rosa

This former farmhouse in the Cilento Hills takes guests
With the bountiful and ready hospitality
Of an *agroturismo* whose invisible state
Subsidies are instantly translated into the
Merry flagging-down of slow drivers only half-lost
On their road at the edge of the great wooded valley,
And the day-long provision of rare home-made fare:
The just-churned ice cream with picked berries, their own
    rosso,
The nine-course meal, paced to the determined appetite
Like a well-instructed team of long-distance runners.

Everything that a farm can provide is found here:
The breads, the jam, the slaughtered beasts, the butter with
    rind.
Even the bubbling water is made from their own well.
The wayfarer yields up his will, and consents to be
Restored to the earth by such extensive exposure,
For tomorrow he will be quickly returned again
To the stamp and brand of the calculating city
Where life is a lawful product like any other
That is counted and costed and assessed, but which has
Neither origin nor individuality.

At the end of the talkative evening, night gives
Its commands and the guests stretch upwards from their
    tables.
Our bedroom window, thrown open for its view which is
Already gathering a mountainish sort of mist,
Lies under the eaves and is a hazard to swallows
Who nest there and circulate madly for night insects.
The strange attraction of our aired and rarely lit room
To the smaller-winged life-forms of the fields about us
Is understandable, and soon we have the raised red
Bites on our knees, like blemishes on fruit, to prove it.

Light itself, in the form of naked bulbs, is fatal
To the moth in the bathroom, still as the Ace of Death.
And in the morning, to the sound of a crowing cock,
A swallow swoops in and out of the room, performing
A brilliant series of prizewinning skating moves
In a rich flicker of cream, buff and ultramarine
Around the grey bulb, looking like an instant lampshade
With moving parts, or a maid come to clear the room of
All six-legged marauders, or a sort of dervish
Casting a marvellous spell on the opening day.

Such a day is fresh as the crimson clover in the
Grass verges, the morning prayer of the gruff working
Dog, the dew beading the wire run for the guinea-fowl.
Waking is to wake as disguised sultans in fables
With all the riches to hand that his people earn for him
In their original and simplest form. When the sun
Finally scales the treetops, the revelation is
Complete, the animals all bathed in their own shadow,
A small cycle finished, the day ready to begin.
The car starts bravely, but the wheel seems heavy to turn.

RUBY

Green, like a beginning thing,
An emerald was my dream of true,
Complete and endless like the ring
   You put your finger through.

And now, after twice twenty years,
Here are two rubies that will stand
Like globes of blood upon your ears
   To match that emerald band.

Ruby and emerald are kin,
Their chromium impurity the same,
The crystal field strength weaker in
   The shoot than in the flame.

From one life to another flows
The charge that gives the future shape,
Its colour to the grass or rose,
   The bloom upon the grape.

Life is distinct, but vanishing.
As I must be, so too will you be
That indistinguishable thing,
   Both emerald and ruby.

THE TONGUE AND THE HEART

A pretty little space between the Tongue & the heart, like that between East & West. Coleridge, *Notebooks*, May 1799

1 Hemispheres

As with the hemispheres,
So between the ears
There is a space we seek
And that is where we speak.

This is what we say.
This is what we feel.
There is a space between,
And that is what we mean.

Love has no East or West,
And surely love knows best
How between tongue and heart
Words must play their part.

And yet this is not all:
Two hemispheres recall
The world where they belong,
The world that is their song.

2 Sunset

Come and look at the sun!
Look at the flagging sun:
Tired of the day he made,
A perfect arch of a day.
He is wrapping it up in the sky
And saving it up for tomorrow.
In these hours of the evening
He thinks he can do better.

A careless teacher, the sun,
Although we dearly love him:
So many days he wastes,
Gathering all the pieces,
Or throwing them away,
Frustrated or in tears.
In these days of our evening
We know we can do better.

3 Pichet

A little jug of wine
   And glasses for two:
Yours, of course, and mine.
   Just for me and you.

Glazed breakable clay
   And full to the spout
On the exciting day
   When we shared it out.

The wine went overboard
   At every tilt
Of the jug we so eagerly poured,
   Reckless of whether it spilled.

Whenever we lifted the jug
   We could not decide
How much of its weight and glug
   There might be left inside.

Though all that we've attempted
   Has come to pass
And the jug nearly emptied,
   There's still wine in the glass.

4 Lizard

He was here before us
And this is his stone.

In the day-long sunshine
Shadow is his home.

His small flanks are dappled
With the ready-made
And myriad concealments
Of light and shade.

Little lick of a tail,
A scamper in the dust,
And no way of counting
The hours as they pass.

We are old sweethearts
With playful language
And fond silence
For camouflage.

Together we take note of
The lizard's calligraphy
Upon his finished stone:
It's his eternity.

5 *Headlands*

Near you always, just a step behind you
    As the headland rises before us
        And the hills tumble to the sea.

And should there be one more after this one
    You will want to walk there for the view.
        And if you, then surely me.

On they extend, as the coast curves ahead:
    A different view of something
        That for a moment has no name.

Look behind you: the distance we've travelled
    Seems too great for the time we've taken.
        For what's to come it is much the same.

6 *Puzzle*

Within my arms there is a space
That aches for you, though you are there
Just over the horizon
Of the passing moment,
Reading a book, or in a chair.

Heads together under the water,
Heads together over sky,
Patient until its edges
Form their promise of
A landscape of the by-and-by.

There is a story in all shape.
There is memory in an embrace.
And things like missing pieces
Eventually turn up
Like love, in their hiding place.

7 *Crossing*

The throbbing deck still warm
To the cautious soles of the feet,
Heads touching at the prow,
Music settled to its beat.

Though the wake may be troubled,
Our course is a smooth curve.
In the still velvet of the air
The vessel holds its nerve.

Onward, steadily,
Onward under the stars!
Fire streaks from the zenith,
Night unlocks her armoires!

POMME

Although the sea, with its senseless political grievance,
Has resumed its recent attempts upon the shore
And a shrapnel of spray falls back upon the rocks
In a careless sluicing, the surface is not unfriendly.
Your flip-flops in the crevice, your launching foot-splash,
The squat breathing-tube, the swell of the maillot,
Reveal that you are still undaunted by the waves.
Behind the glass of your aquarium headpiece
The underseascape is a framed display,
A locked stare, as from a *dix-huitième*
Scaphandre, at an unfamiliar salon
Whose hosts are welcoming, though a trifle insolent.

Here is a slow bogue making cow-eyes, and
Suddenly changing direction like a dodgem.
Boops boops! The alarm is not absolute,
Just nature's instinct for the preferred soup.
Here are couched urchins, snugly comfortable
In the privilege of protection by Mayor Casasoprana.
Here is a mobile of squirlu nodding for crumbs
That escape from the squelched crust in your swimming fist.
They point, not exactly in the same direction,
But in a casual variety of angles that define
The distant point that may be in their thoughts,
Like an effort in perspective by Uccello.

The mind, moving over metres like the deity
Of the water's painted ceiling, a shadow in the light,
Makes of itself what it will: a blankness lulled
By recent waking, a contented sculling over
Dreamscape; or a beneficent enquiring spirit
Noting the plutonic shelving, the mossed gabbros
And eroded diorite, like ancient unwashed dishes,
And constructing a slow history of patient collapse
On this unchanging shore. Its only witness
Is the noise of waves, the planet's primal song,

The clamour of water frustrated at a threshold,
A plea of sorts, a luxurious performance.

You hear it all the time, behind all other sounds,
Even in sleep, when it is most like the voices
Which, if you could only manage to hear them,
Are ready to expound your deepest thoughts.
Put aside your calculations then,
Coast with the swell and dip, the sudden chill
Or warmth of the currents, the sound of your own
    breathing.
Let this pale otherworld lead you on and on
Through colder and bluer depths to some vision
Of an absolute, the dream-words still in the head
And hard to shake off, *comme de bien entendu.*

I will follow, as I always have done, and will do.
Of our many private performances, this is the freshest,
Our courses idly circling and meeting for a moment
In soundless acknowledgement. The sea stands for
Something that is always felt in the blood and breathing
Of our bodily lives. It is always in wait for us,
Pomme, for you are Pomme here, a little more carefree,
A bobbing, floating persona, concentrated in perception,
Full of your tenderest thoughts, Pomme, gazing out,
Graceful in water, striking from the shore,
Named by friends misreading your name in a letter,
Named in explicable error, callionymous Pomme.

And when the lightning begins to describe the mountains
With its startled flicker, the clouds are affronted,
The mistral blowing, the inky sea on horseback,
And we wonder what the fishes can find to do
As the gallons roll and split upon the bay.
The shutters, though shut, stutter through the night,
The wind shaking the house like an old box,
Not quite fooled into believing that it is empty.
It makes a bid to invade our secret dreams

Where we lie prone in great drama while the clock
Faithfully records the unnoticed times
Of these encounters with an alternative past.

Whatever the outcome of these broken narratives
Of wish and betrayal in the peopled inland
Of the mind, whatever the vexing forgottenness
Of their intriguing moods and premises,
We know that in the morning all will be still.
In the morning the sea will be whispering again:
'Pomme, Pomme!' After the storm, loosened weed
Is gathered in the rocks, the slim shoals feeding,
The sun stealthy over the eastern mountains,
Pebbles sharp in the light, and always the whispers:
'Pomme, Pomme!' And down you will go to the water,
The apple of my summer life.